THIS CANDLEWICK BIOGRAPHY BELONGS TO:

In honor of Woody Freeman

Henry Aaron's Dream

Matt Tavares

CANDLEWICK PRESS

TABLE OF CONTENTS

CHAPTER ONE

Henry Aaron had a dream.

He wanted to be a big-league baseball player.

He didn't have a bat,
so he'd swing a broom handle
or a stick
or whatever he could find.

Henry didn't have a baseball, either,
so he'd hit bottle caps
or tie a few old rags together
or crumple up a tin can.

Henry liked to play in his yard
and imagine himself in the big leagues.

But his father knew he shouldn't get his hopes up.
"Ain't no colored ballplayers," he told Henry.

Still, Henry held on to his dream.

In the 1940s in Mobile, Alabama,
it was against the law
for black kids and white kids
to play baseball together.
There were baseball diamonds all over the city,
but they all had signs that said
WHITES ONLY.

When Henry was twelve,
the city of Mobile opened Carver Park—
the only baseball field in the whole city
with a sign that said
COLORED ONLY.

That's where Henry spent his days.
He'd race to the park after school
and play ball with his friends
until it was too dark to see.

Henry loved playing on a real baseball field,
with real bats and real baseballs.
He was small and skinny,
and he held the bat the wrong way—
he batted right-handed,
with his left hand on top.
But he practiced and practiced
until he could hit the ball harder
than any of the other kids at Carver Park.

CHAPTER TWO

On April 15, 1947, when Henry was thirteen,
Jackie Robinson played his first game
for the Brooklyn Dodgers.
Finally, there was a black ballplayer
in the big leagues.

Henry's whole world changed.

He kept playing ball at Carver Park
and dreaming of making it to the majors.
Only now, thanks to Jackie Robinson,
he knew his dream could come true.

Henry started listening
to every Dodger game on the radio
and reading every article he could find
about Jackie Robinson.
Henry learned what Jackie was going through.

Everywhere Jackie played,
white fans called him terrible names.
Some even sent him letters,
threatening to kill him if he kept playing.
Opposing players spiked him with their cleats.
Even some of his own teammates
refused to play ball with a black man.

**And through it all,
Jackie persevered.**

He played hard every day and showed the world
that he was just as good as anyone.

CHAPTER THREE

After spring training in 1948,
Jackie Robinson and the Dodgers
came to Mobile
to play an exhibition game at Hartwell Field.
Henry's father took him to the game.

**There he was—
number forty-two—
Jackie Robinson.**

Henry was mesmerized.
He watched his hero's every move.
Sitting in the colored section,
way out in right field,
Henry told his father that someday soon,
he'd be out there playing ball with Jackie.

Three years later, in 1951,
the manager of the Mobile Black Bears,
a local semi-pro team,
saw Henry playing at Carver Park
and asked him to join the team.

Henry was still in high school,
and his mother didn't want him
traveling around with a baseball team.
So he only played home games, and only on Sundays.
He got paid ten dollars after every game,
and he even got his own uniform.

That same year,
the Dodgers held a tryout camp
for black ballplayers in Mobile.

Kids from all over the city came to try out,
all hoping to become the next Jackie Robinson.
When it was Henry's turn to bat,
he took his best swings,
but the Dodger scouts were not impressed.
All they saw was a skinny kid
who held his bat the wrong way.
They told him he was too small,
and Henry went back home.

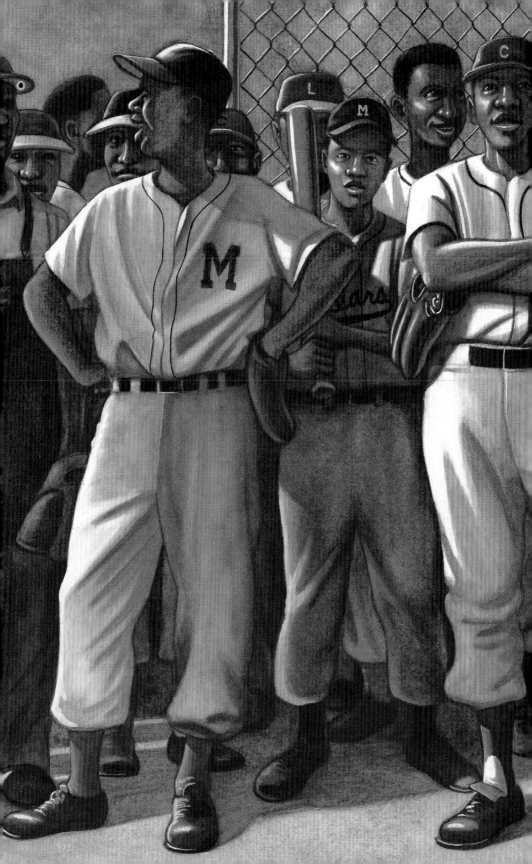

CHAPTER FOUR

Still, Henry didn't give up his dream.
In 1952, after he finished high school,
he started playing shortstop
for the Indianapolis Clowns
in the Negro Leagues.

Most of the black ballplayers in the majors,
like Larry Doby, Monte Irvin, and
Jackie Robinson,
had been discovered while
playing in the Negro Leagues.
**Henry thought this
might be his best chance.**

Watching him play, Henry's teammates knew
he wouldn't be in the Negro Leagues for long.
He was so talented and so young—
just what big-league teams were looking for.
His teammates knew this all too well.

They were older. Some of them
had been playing in the Negro Leagues
for ten or fifteen years.
They had watched so many
of their younger teammates
leave for the majors and become stars
while they stayed behind.

They slept on buses every night,
arriving at a new city each morning,
almost never stopping to eat at a restaurant,
because so few restaurants would serve them.

Back when they were Henry's age,
they used to dream of making it
to the major leagues,
but by the time Jackie Robinson
signed with the Dodgers,
it was already too late for them.
Big-league teams just weren't looking for
thirty-five-year-old rookies
from the Negro Leagues.

One rainy day in Buffalo,
after the first game of a doubleheader,
a scout for the Braves approached Henry
and asked if he would try
batting with his right hand on top.
In his next at-bat, Henry switched his hands
and hit a home run over the right-field fence.

A few days later, the Braves —
a real big-league team! —
offered him a minor-league contract.
Henry packed his cardboard suitcase,
said good-bye to his teammates,
and boarded a northbound train.

CHAPTER FIVE

He joined the Braves' Class C minor-league team
in Eau Claire, Wisconsin.

Henry was nervous before his first game—
**he had never faced
a white pitcher before.**
He had been told for a long time that
white ballplayers were better
than black ballplayers.

In his first at-bat, he lined a single into left field.
As soon as he heard that familiar *crack!*
when his bat hit the ball,
he knew he was going to be okay.

In 1953, Henry spent another season in the minors,
but he was promoted to the Class A team
in Jacksonville, Florida.
He had two black teammates,
Horace Garner and Felix Mantilla.
The rest of the team was white.

Before that season, no black player
had ever played in the South Atlantic League.
They played their games in southern cities
where black people and white people
weren't even allowed to play checkers together.

Some white fans called Henry terrible names.
Some even sent him letters, threatening to kill him if he kept playing.
Some fans stopped coming to games.
Some of the fans who came threw rocks at him.
Pitchers fired fastballs at his head.

Henry didn't understand why they hated him.
All he wanted to do was play baseball.

Sometimes it got to him.
But then he remembered Jackie Robinson
and all he had gone through to pave the way.
And he remembered his teammates from the Negro Leagues,
who never got the chance to live their dream.

Henry focused on the ball
and tried to ignore everything else.

CHAPTER SIX

Every game, wherever the team played,
the colored section was packed with fans.
They came to watch Henry, Horace, and Felix.

Playing second base, Henry could hear them
cheering wildly for every routine play.
He remembered the day back in Mobile
when he'd sat in the colored section
and watched Jackie Robinson.
He knew how much it meant to these people
to watch him play.
He was more determined than ever
to make his dream come true.

Henry played so well that season
that by the end of the year,
some of the white fans
who had stopped coming to games
came back to the ballpark.
Some of them even cheered for him.

The night Jacksonville won the pennant,
the team had a big party
at a restaurant in Savannah,
but only white people were allowed in.

While the other players celebrated,
the Most Valuable Player, Henry Aaron,
sat in the kitchen with Horace and Felix
and waited until the party was over.

That winter, Henry played ball in Puerto Rico,
where he faced real big-league pitchers.
For the first time ever, he struggled at the plate.
And he made so many errors at second base
that his manager switched him to the outfield.

Back at home, even though Henry was still
on the minor-league roster,
he got to travel with the big-league club
for the first few spring training games in 1954.
The Braves' starters played
the first five or six innings of each game,
then minor-leaguers like Henry would take over.
Henry knew that any day
he would be sent back to the minors,
so he made the most of every at-bat.

During the second game of spring training,
the Braves' starting center fielder
sprained his ankle.
The next day, his replacement pulled a muscle.
Suddenly the Braves needed outfielders.

On March 10, when Henry checked the lineup
for the spring training game
versus the Boston Red Sox,
he couldn't believe it:

**he was starting in right field
and batting leadoff.**

Henry hit a home run that day,
and for the next three weeks,
he never left the starting lineup.

CHAPTER SEVEN

On the last day of spring training,
Henry signed his first real major-league contract.
The regular season was just a few days away.

Henry's dream was about to come true.

On their way north from spring training,
the Braves stopped in Mobile
to play an exhibition game at Hartwell Field
against the Brooklyn Dodgers.

The colored section was packed.
Henry's mother and father, aunts and uncles,
sisters and brothers, neighbors and friends
all came to the game.
Old friends shared stories about
how they used to play ball
with Henry at Carver Park.

When Henry came up to bat,
he could hear the fans in the colored section
cheering and clapping and shouting his name.

Henry smacked a line drive into left field.
He hustled around first and slid into second,
just beating the throw from the left fielder,
his hero, Jackie Robinson.

"SAFE!" yelled the umpire.

Henry Aaron had a dream.

He wanted to be a big-league baseball player.

There were times when it seemed almost impossible

and times when he almost gave up,

but finally, one fine day in 1954,

Henry Aaron's dream came true.

‖ Author's Note

During that trip north after spring training in 1954, the black players on the Braves and Dodgers stayed at the same hotels. In the evenings, Don Newcombe, Roy Campanella, Joe Black, and other players gathered in Jackie Robinson's room to play cards and discuss the challenges they faced as black ballplayers. The civil rights movement was just beginning, and those players would be instrumental in the fight against racism — in baseball and in America. Henry Aaron sat in the corner and listened, taking it all in.

During Aaron's rookie season with the Braves, everyone started calling him "Hank." Hank Aaron quickly became one of the best all-around players in the major leagues. At the peak of his fame, he followed Jackie Robinson's lead and began speaking out about the racial injustice he faced in baseball.

During spring training in 1961, he fought to have all race-related signs removed from the Braves' ballpark and pressured Braves' management to find a hotel that would the accept the entire team as its guests — white players and black players alike.

Late in his career, as Hank Aaron closed in on Babe Ruth's all-time home-run record, he received thousands of hateful letters and death threats from people who did not want a black man to become baseball's home-run king. By then, Jackie Robinson had already passed away, but Aaron was determined to keep Robinson's dream alive. He tried his best to ignore all the hatred and prove to everyone that there was no limit to what a black ballplayer could accomplish. On April 8, 1974, Hank Aaron went deep for the 715th time, surpassing Babe Ruth's all-time record.

When he retired, in 1976, Hank Aaron was the league's all-time leader, with 755 home runs. He ranked first in runs batted in, total bases, and extra base hits, and third in runs and hits. During his career, he won two batting titles and three Gold Glove Awards.

In 1999, Major League Baseball announced a new award given to the best hitter in each league. They named it the Hank Aaron Award. In 2009, Henry Aaron was honored with the Beacon of Life Award, which is given by Major League Baseball to an individual who embodies the spirit of the civil rights movement.

Henry Aaron's rookie card, 1954

‖ Bibliography

Aaron, Hank. "After Jackie." *Time,* April 12, 2007.

——— with Dick Schapp. *Home Run: My Life in Pictures.* Kingston, NY: Total Sports, 1999.

——— with Lonnie Wheeler. *I Had a Hammer: The Hank Aaron Story.* New York: HarperCollins, 1991.

AP. "Braves Lose Second in Row to Dodgers." *Stevens Point* (Wisconsin) *Daily Journal,* April 2, 1954, p. 6.

Ethier, Bryan. "Hank Aaron: Interview with the Former Atlanta Braves Slugger." *American History,* June 1999.

Hirshberg, Al. *Henry Aaron, Quiet Superstar.* New York: Putnam, 1969.

Jacobson, Steve. *Carrying Jackie's Torch: The Players Who Integrated Baseball — and America.* Chicago: Lawrence Hill Books, 2007.

McCormick, Henry J. "Red Sox Hand Braves Second Straight Loss." *Wisconsin State Journal,* March 11, 1954. Sports Section, p.1.

Peterson, Robert. *Only the Ball Was White.* Englewood Cliffs, NJ: Prentice-Hall, 1970.

Robinson, Jackie, and Alfred Duckett, *I Never Had It Made: An Autobiography of Jackie Robinson.* New York: Putnam, 1972.

Stanton, Tom. *Hank Aaron and the Home Run that Changed America.* New York: William Morrow, 2004.

Stewart, Mark, and Mike Kennedy. *Hammering Hank: How the Media Made Henry Aaron.* Guilford, CT: Lyons Press, 2006.

Ward, Geoffrey C., and Ken Burns. *Baseball: An Illustrated History.* New York: Knopf, 1994.

This statue of Henry Aaron hitting his 715th home run is located in Monument Park, just outside of Turner Field, the Braves' home stadium. It was sculpted by Ed Dwight Jr. and dedicated on September 7, 1982.

HENRY LOUIS AARON

Height: 6 feet; Weight: 180 lbs.; Born: February 5, 1934; Mobile, Alabama

YEAR	TEAM	G	AB	R	H
1952	Indianapolis Clowns	26	ND	ND	41
1952	Eau Claire	87	345	79	116
1953	Jacksonville	137	574	115	208
1954	Milwaukee Braves	122	468	58	131
1955	Milwaukee Braves	153	602	105	189
1956	Milwaukee Braves	153	609	106	200
1957	Milwaukee Braves	151	615	118	198
1958	Milwaukee Braves	153	601	109	196
1959	Milwaukee Braves	154	629	116	223
1960	Milwaukee Braves	153	590	102	172
1961	Milwaukee Braves	155	603	115	197
1962	Milwaukee Braves	156	592	127	191
1963	Milwaukee Braves	161	631	121	201
1964	Milwaukee Braves	145	570	103	187
1965	Milwaukee Braves	150	570	109	181
1966	Atlanta Braves	158	603	117	168
1967	Atlanta Braves	155	600	113	184
1968	Atlanta Braves	160	606	84	174
1969	Atlanta Braves	147	547	100	164
1970	Atlanta Braves	150	516	103	154
1971	Atlanta Braves	139	495	95	162
1972	Atlanta Braves	129	449	75	119
1973	Atlanta Braves	120	392	84	118
1974	Atlanta Braves	112	340	47	91
1975	Milwaukee Brewers	137	465	45	109
1976	Milwaukee Brewers	85	271	22	62
MLB Career		**3,298**	**12,364**	**2,174**	**3,771**

Key: G = Games, R = Runs, H = Hits, 2B = Doubles, 3B = Triples, HR = Home Runs, RBI = Runs Batted In, SB = Stolen Bases, AVG = Batting Average, SLG = Slugging Percentage, ND = No Data

2B	3B	HR	RBI	SB	AVG	SLG
ND	ND	5	33	9	.366	ND
19	4	9	61	ND	.336	.493
36	14	22	125	ND	.362	.589
27	6	13	69	2	.280	.447
37	9	27	106	3	.314	.540
34	14	26	92	2	.328	.558
27	6	44	132	1	.322	.600
34	4	30	95	4	.326	.546
46	7	39	123	8	.355	.636
20	11	40	126	16	.292	.566
39	10	34	120	21	.327	.594
28	6	45	128	15	.323	.618
29	4	44	130	31	.319	.586
30	2	24	95	22	.328	.514
40	1	32	89	24	.318	.560
23	1	44	127	21	.279	.539
37	3	39	109	17	.307	.573
33	4	29	86	28	.287	.498
30	3	44	97	9	.300	.607
26	1	38	118	9	.298	.574
22	3	47	118	1	.327	.669
10	0	34	77	4	.265	.514
12	1	40	96	1	.301	.643
16	0	20	69	1	.268	.491
16	2	12	60	0	.234	.355
8	0	10	35	0	.229	.369
624	98	755	2,297	240	.305	.555

The Braves franchise has called three different cities home since its inception into the National League: Boston (1876 – 1953), Milwaukee (1953 – 1965), and Atlanta (1965 – present).

∥ INDEX

Negro Leagues, 12–15, 20

Newcombe, Don, 34

segregation, 24

semi-pro team, 10

shortstop, 12

South Atlantic League, 19

outfield, 24, 27

starting lineup, 27

statistics, 36–37

practice, 1–2, 5

Puerto Rico, 24

threats, 7, 20, 34

racism, 34

records and awards, 24, 34

Red Sox, 27

retirement, 34

right field, 27

Robinson, Jackie, 5–7, 9, 12, 15, 20,
    23, 30, 34

Ruth, Babe, 34

Savannah, Georgia, 24

scouts, 10, 15

second base, 23, 24

MATT TAVARES is the author-illustrator of *Zachary's Ball*, *Oliver's Game*, *Mudball*, *There Goes Ted Williams*, and *Becoming Babe Ruth*. He is also the illustrator of *Iron Hans*, *'Twas the Night Before Christmas*, *Jack and the Beanstalk*, Doreen Rappaport's *Lady Liberty*, and Kristin Kladstrup's *The Gingerbread Pirates*. About *Henry Aaron's Dream*, he says, "When I set out to write about Henry Aaron, I expected to focus on his historic quest to break Major League Baseball's all-time home-run record. But in researching his life, I found that the most fascinating part of Henry Aaron's story took place before he ever set foot on a Major League Baseball field—back when he was a skinny kid who held his bat the wrong way and who never gave up his dream of becoming a big-league baseball player even when it seemed impossible." Matt Tavares lives in Ogunquit, Maine.